ROYAL EAGLE

Miracle of Inner Freedom & Peace

Discover yourself – Update yourself A new philosophy

Copyright © 2023 by Royal Eagle

All rights reserved. No part of this publication may be reproduced, stored or transmitted in any form or by any means, electronic, mechanical, photocopying, recording, scanning, or otherwise without written permission from the publisher. It is illegal to copy this book, post it to a website, or distribute it by any other means without permission.

Royal Eagle asserts the moral right to be identified as the author of this work.

Royal Eagle has no responsibility for the persistence or accuracy of URLs for external or third-party Internet Websites referred to in this publication and does not guarantee that any content on such Websites is, or will remain, accurate or appropriate.

Designations used by companies to distinguish their products are often claimed as trademarks. All brand names and product names used in this book and on its cover are trade names, service marks, trademarks and registered trademarks of their respective owners. The publishers and the book are not associated with any product or vendor mentioned in this book. None of the companies referenced within the book have endorsed the book.

First edition

This book was professionally typeset on Reedsy. Find out more at reedsy.com

This book is dedicated to everyone

Even war is peaceful when it is done willingly and wholeheartedly.

If ambition is strong.. even death seems very small.

Wanting security is what makes us without security.

The world will not stop because you have a problem now.. Problems are not only for you but for everyone. Life is not only for you but for everyone.

No matter how many methods you follow, no matter how many principles you follow, no change will happen if there is no realization in you..

Royal Eagle

Contents

Preface		ii
1	Description	1
2	Truth	3
3	Change	5
4	Meditation	9
5	Fear	12
6	Peace	14
7	Motivation & Positive Thinking	18
8	Competition & Comparison	24
9	Energy Loss due to Conflict & Unnecessary things	27
10	Confusion	30
11	Condition	34
12	Depression	42
13	Freedom	45
14	Missing Present	50
15	Trap	55
16	Growth	59
17	Life	68
18	Love	71
19	Stories	74

Preface

In this book all the chapters are written topic wise. Each and every topic has it's own conclusion and it's own specialty. As per topic situation and for more understanding very few sentence are repeated. All topics were simplified as much as possible and each and every topic is very important. This book has been written with many new things that no one has seen or heard. Many topics does not make sense if there is a prior intention.

1

Description

When the path is full of fog, the path is not clear and thoughts like fog also make life unclear and meaningless. This book is a small part of the effort to remove the foggy thoughts. This world means one thing to one person and another thing to another person. It depends on their mental condition and their condition. But there is a different world to be understood, and if it is understood, the world will look different. This book is an attempt to say that.

Even if you go to a beautiful place with a conditioned mind, it will be like a leftover task. Even the grass is beautiful when there is no condition. Life is the same. And talking about peace, Even War is peaceful when it is done willingly and wholeheartedly. Why aren't we mindful? To be understood.

Sometimes one does not know the way to face the enemy but the same enemy indirectly shows the way to face himself. This world shows many paths if you have to put your mind to it...

This book has been written with many new things that no one has seen or heard. This is a book for everyone. It makes sense if read very carefully. Life will be different if you know and understand some things beforehand. Realization is at the end of life and then there is no use if you think that you have missed a lot in life. In this book all the chapters are written topic wise. Each and every topic has it's own conclusion and it's own specialty. Many topics does not make sense if there is a prior intention.

2

Truth

Truth example story: Once upon a time in one kingdom one person found truth. Some people who noticed it, without listening to what he said, forcefully brought it from him and put it in one place, shouted loudly and created a huge scene and formed it into a company. They want to give it to everyone. Later they realized that what they wanted to bring did not come with them, only its traces. It doesn't make sense, they don't have anything to do, they gave a little touch up to it and gave it to everyone. Everyone thought that many miracles are going to happen in their lives. But then a few days passed and they realize that the old conditions are still the same. Yet they realize that there is no change, that what was once there still continued, what happened was the same but only the name has changed. Some others who noticed all that have now formed an even bigger organization. They are very skilled in finishing touches, and it is advertised that they have the best quality. Now they strongly believe that miracles are going to happen in their lives. But after a few days, the old situation will be found again. Truth is not distributed by one to another, it does not stay in one place, and what one knows does not work for another, until no one has the meaning to know for themselves, so it will continue.

Topic-2: When we have a problem, naturally thinking is different from understanding. But it is different to imagine problems that we don't have or to know other people's problems and think that they should not come to us. That would be starting a new problem that we don't have. There is no solution for such things. Because that's not really a problem, it's one we've made ourselves. Also, huge efforts are being made all over the world for solutions to these self-imposed problems. Such is the truth-seeking. Truth is not preconceived, not foreknown, and not somewhere far away. It is not something that becomes something else and becomes known. It is a complete lie that we are searching for the truth and that we have come to know the truth. What is the search for truth? It is not a hidden treasure. Truth is not something to seek. Or it is not known once, it is not yet happened. To put it plainly, truth was always living, changing moment by moment, always knowing. Once you get on the bus, it is not like you have traveled enough for life, it is not like you have reached the coast.

3

Change

No matter how much you talk about light while sitting in darkness, it will not become light, it is all part of darkness. And no matter how many opinions about it, it doesn't seem to have changed, they are all good as they are. Whatever is made is nothing other than itself, but even if it is named light, what happens is old. Memories take different forms but are all part of it. To put it more easily.. If you tell someone not to take bribe. Ok I will stop taking it but how much will you give me for stopping?. Is it like talking about a new contract? Here bribery has become a different type, nothing has changed here. The direction changed and it was the same again. Almost all our changes are like this. Here when what is not wanted is a small part of what is wanted.. what is not wanted does not have the power to take away what is wanted because it is born from it. There is no change; whatever happens in different forms remains the same. Change by desire is a lie. Coming out with full understanding is different, it's new, it's not longed for, and memories don't work as well. It is different when the thought starts with a completely understood and different perspective.

Topic-2: Are you expecting something new to happen now!?. That's what I thought all these years. Did any miracles happen!?. At least now I want to see if I can think of something new. I have also done the same till now but now I want to think anew. Many years have already been wasted. The decision we take works well when it is well understood and inbuilt in our daily activities. Or being motivated and promising something passionately means that it is not related to our present state. It clearly means something else. That is why it always remains irrelevant to us. That is why one thing is said and one thing is done. To put it clearly, a promise is a part that is split from the present situation and then merges back into it again. When what is not wanted is part of what is wanted, what is not wanted has no power to take away what is wanted. Otherwise, one should fully understand and throw everything aside and think that he is a king. Then there is the possibility of a new start. What is made of a well when it is in it is part of it, but not something else. Coming to the shore is different, it is new, and there are no memories of the old. There are similar reasons for not starting even some plans made for the future.

Topic-3: No matter how many methods you follow, no matter how many principles you follow, no change will happen if there is no realization in you..

Topic-4: Just like light and darkness do not go together.. positive and negative also do not go together. We want to change one thing to another but it is not possible. When there is light there is no darkness, when there is darkness there is no light. They are two separate things. We want to change negative thoughts into positive ones.. but is it really possible?.. It is never like that. When one does not exist, the other exists. Changing does not mean controlling, changing does not mean putting make-up on what is. Otherwise, everything will change if you understand and come out.

Topic-5: If you don't have the intention to change, no matter how many words you say, how many quotations you read, and how many books you read, it will not be of much use. Not a single thing can influence you. It's a lie that something else moves you because you're in the business of accumulating them and you've turned it into a habit, you've turned it into an addiction. And you want something new in them, but you don't want to be new, you don't want to change. I don't understand what are you waiting for?

Topic-6: Everyone in the world wants to change but in some situations they just don't know how. There are some things that are done on purpose, and some that are done unintentionally. A habit, good or bad, has the same effect on the mind. Conflict in any mind! Example: When a habit is covered like a banyan tree.. When the one who wants to change is like a seed that falls from that tree, how does that seed have the power to remove that tree?. However, that seed also has the same characteristics but how do you expect it to have different characteristics?, because it also came from it, it also has the same characteristics. It's the love you have for it that makes it so. Why do you think differently now? It looks like you are trying to imagine something after listening to someone's words, but do you really want to change? Have you ever thought about it? If you really think about it, you will get the power to remove not only the tree but also the roots. In other words, we are looking for the solution within the problem. There is a problem within the problem but no solution. The solution lies elsewhere. When a tool to remove a problem is made with the problem itself, it works in favor of the problem but how can it work against it?...Until some things don't make sense, it will remain the same until we change our way of thinking.

Topic-7: Changing does not mean controlling.. understanding and getting out. Everything has changed with understanding.. You know that! But why do you want to separate with old memories and change there again?.. You should know.

4

Meditation

Meditation is not about leaving the shining world and going into a dark cave and looking for light in that place. Separation is a trick. That state, figuratively speaking, is not light, not dark, not far, not near, not high, not deep, not angry, not sad, not happy, not sad, not difficult, not happy, not relinquished, not wanting. That's all it will be. It is the stillness at the bottom of an ocean that nothing touches it, nothing clings to it. If you try for it, it will not come, that effort will separate you again. It should be understood by those who are themselves.

Topic-2: - Empty of traffic: Conflict in our mind is something we create. Because of contradiction we cannot see the whole, we can only see in parts. While viewing one, the other hides, while viewing the other, the first hides. Sometimes when you see one, you only imagine that something else is there, but it may not be there. Contradiction is the reason why the mind does not see something completely but only partially. Example: Summer season and winter season are not two opposites, birth and death are not two opposites, happiness and unhappiness are not two opposites, light and darkness are not two opposites, morning and evening are not two opposites.. They are all two aspects of the same process. All of them meet side by side like a valley mountain. But the mind perceives differently, feeds differently and creates conflict. Some things are clearly understood and the mind's influence is reduced.. When meditation arises, it sees everything as a whole, it does not feel against each other, it is one with everything. And we are always confused and choose something. But if we choose something, immediately something else is invited into our mind. It haunts like a shadow.. The conflict between the two begins. When you choose happiness, you get unhappiness, when you want success, failure is like a shadow, when you have hopes, frustration waits, if you strive for life, you get death, if you want friendship, you get enmity, if you want happiness, you get pain, if you want to think positively, you get negative. All of them are like two sides of the same coin and create a paradox. If you choose one, the other will be like a shadow at its back end.. When you observe the unity of life observing that it is all there is oneness with everything. If you realize that truth, everything will fly away and you will start to understand what it is. Then gradually stop choosing. Choosing one stops. One is left with no choice. All contradictions cease when there is no choice. Lies can be chosen but the truth cannot be chosen, the truth is already there, nothing has to do with it. It is only to understand it.. and it has nothing to do with liking, disliking, choosing. As certain things continue to make sense, the ideas become more focused. If you observe those thoughts and realize their source, they will start to diminish. The thoughts that are in excess will slowly decrease, and their speed will also decrease. Then the vacancies start coming. Then a thought goes by and another thought doesn't come for a long time. After a while the thoughts disappear for hours. just empty of traffic. That is, unnecessary thoughts do not come, they come and go when they are needed. It is calm and there is no giving up. Then the mind becomes even more sharp.

Topic-3: It is a mistake if we create something for our satisfaction and change it like a habit and think that it is meditation. What is meditation? Why should we meditate? We practice something because someone told us it will do us good. But practice is repeated. By doing it repeatedly it becomes mechanical.. There is nothing but strain in it. Straining means it is not meditation. We want to remove existing problems with meditation, but that is not a tool to remove problems. Problems are always there and new ones are always coming. Example: When you are hungry, does meditation satisfy your hunger? Also the problems are not solved. Doing so is like escaping from the situation. Meditation is not something that can be achieved separately. Before learning about a subject there are different types of thoughts but after learning about it the mind becomes calm in that particular subject. Also, having an understanding about life and problems, thoughts should be reduced overall. Not to control. It will never happen without problems but they should be understood. To be clear, the problem is not separate, we are not separate. We are the problem. But when you try to separate, it seems to be escaping! The solution to the problem is somewhere else.. there is a big gap. The problem is we are the same, we think about the problem seriously when we think about it. Some meaningful thoughts are less effective. Part of meditation is to think about and understand the problems and their roots.

5

Fear

Fear plays a major role in our lives. Sometimes it is unbearable and makes no sense. Yet separates us from ourselves. It always acts as a reason for an unknown thing. To put it more clearly, it comes from tying the known past to the unknown future. It is created by thinking that the bitterness of the past should not come again in the future, or that the good things happened in the past should also be in the future. Once in a while, because of the feeling of being scared for no reason, some old memories are created reminding you to do the same thing again. No event in life is equal to another event. Everything is new. But some things do not make sense and have to remain in confusion for a long time. Fear really doesn't have the power to change reality, it's not reality but it's all encompassing and doesn't let things go so easily. Death is inevitable but thoughts about it and fear cannot stop it. We analyze to get rid of fear but in that process one side decreases and another side creates a new one, it is an endless process. Whatever is done is of no use. If you yearn for good, you are afraid that bad will come. If you crave for something else, you are afraid that it will be something else. The problem is due to the desire to be different without understanding the situation here. But if all that happens is understood as a whole and the reality is recognized, that will be the end.

Topic-2: What is the cause of fear? We want to let go of that, understand only fear and get rid of it. But it cannot. Because fear is not individual in itself, it does not exist on its own, it depends on other things and is linked with other things. It cannot be understood without proper understanding of what causes it. Without knowing it. After analyzing it well, you will find out what kind of fear it is, how dangerous it is, or its outline, its trends, and its consequences, and you will know how easily you can explain fear in many ways.. In the end, many books will be written on it, but it will be impossible to get rid of it in the end. It will be the same.. In other words, all the other problems will also be the same. Because they have forgotten to understand the source of the problem. There is fear about a thing, but if you want to let go of that thing and understand the fear itself, it is not possible. Example: There is fear of death. Let's stop living here and think about fear, it's not a solution. If you want to be brave from now on, it means sending an invitation to fear. It is not a problem as long as we don't care too much about a thing but we invite it by thinking the same thing over and over again.. that becomes a problem. Anything is as long as its origins are not understood.

Topic-3: Naturally negative thoughts do not have that much power. But fear makes them powerful. That is why we must first understand fear.

6

Peace

Peace is a property not to be earned. We want to be calm, we want to achieve calmness through desire, but that desire is what makes us not calm. Because if there is desire there is no peace. Peace is not something to be desired, it is not to be achieved. So there is no need to give up desires. When we have the power to understand certain things, when we come to understand ourselves, there is peace without wanting to be there for everything.

Topic-2: Even War is peaceful when it is done willingly and wholeheartedly. When we are mindful, there are no thoughts that separate us from us, no thoughts that oppose us. And thoughts cannot be separated from thoughts and control those thoughts. Peace does not mean being empty and calm while controlling everything. There is peace when you are fully immersed in a task. Then there is single thought in which there is no separation, opposition or control. Why aren't we mindful? To be understood.

Topic-3: Peace: If we leave aside the peace outside, it is about the peace inside us. Fighting is very peaceful when it is done willingly and wholeheartedly. If you are willing, you will be very peaceful even in anger. From childhood someone told us something and we always practice it. Let's stop all thoughts for a while and feel the same peace. Here is thought that stops all thoughts. Some thoughts are separated from thoughts that cease to be thoughts. There are comings and goings in it, everything in it is conflict. And to be clear, who among us is not calm? Who wants to keep who calm?. Without correct understanding of what needs to be understood, no matter how many efforts are made, it will not be of much use. And some go to many places, but where it cannot be found, it remains within us. It is very practice to let go of anger, desires, rage and many more... for peace. But anger, pain, happiness, sadness, love.. these are rare qualities that come naturally to us and they are all wonderful. Without understanding them, we reject everything and do what we have with nothing. We will name it peace. Serenity is not something that can be achieved in isolation. If the thing is understood clearly, it will always be with us in everything. There is calmness when one is fully engaged in a task, whether it be quarrelsome, angry, or whatever. It means not having any other idea where it is not necessary, but not giving up and controlling. To put it simply, if we think that we should sleep peacefully and work peacefully, it means that we are very serious about them, so there is no other way to think. That is what peace means.

Topic-4: A machine in a problem can never make good things! A mind full of violence and confusion will never make a good society. Why do we want everything to change without us changing? Will it give us an effect later!. As we are, so will the next generations be made. Whatever applies to us, it must start with us or it will remain the same. Only those who are at peace can bring about a peaceful empire.

Topic-5: It can be peaceful until there is no problem. Some people remain calm even if there is a problem, they have more awareness.. They know what to do when. But sometimes we think of some things for safety without any problem, but they are not useful when the original problem occurs. We also think that if we take other people's problems, how can we deal with them? Or if we are, we will be different. Some trials also happen in the mind. But that's a useless thing that we don't get. It should be understood that whose life is theirs and whose problems are theirs. When a problem arises, if you think about it according to the situation, you will find the correct solution. But to what extent is it correct to find a solution and wait for the problem? Or how correct is it to create problems that we have some solutions? Ever invented things are old and don't suit new problems. Moreover, all the problems that are coming now are updated and coming with the new version, and the ones that come later may also be updated. That is why the earlier inventions are not so useful. In confusion, we accumulate such things like treasurers, but they are all wasted and the current work stops..

Topic-6: What is peace? Why do we want to be calm? Does serenity mean putting everything aside and becoming an inert substance? Or leave everything and walk away? If you really do that, what is in it? This is what we achieved by wanting to be calm. Is it all peaceful? Eg: Some animals do not rest when their children come near.. If they do not do something to protect the children, they do not have peace of mind.. They try to face for peace. When a kingdom is invaded by enemy kings, that kingdom's king and soldiers fight heroically to save the people. If the king's soldiers do not try to protect the people, they will not have peace of mind. Will do anything for peace. If the freedom fighters left everything and were empty, then there was no peace of mind, their conscience did not agree, they fought for freedom, that was peace for them. If something is happening to our children, do we sit back and think of the same calmness? Will we really have peace of mind then? Why do we expect something that is not useful? They should know who it is. Tranquility is the absence of conflict in the mind. It is quarrel, anger, laughing, pain, crying.. (If you understand them, they will be under control) Make sure that there is no quarrel in your mind, that is peace. There are other people who take care of outside things.. First, understand why there is a conflict in your mind. Letting go is never a peace. Tranquility is being at one with all, being wise in reality.

Topic-7: The role of parents in this world is very amazing. The world is like this because every parent is working hard for their children and fulfilling their responsibilities. If it didn't happen this world would still be very confused, very turbulent.

7

Motivation & Positive Thinking

Why do we always need motivation? Why do you always want something? It means that there is some problem in us. That's why we always want something, otherwise we don't do anything. Our whole life is enough with efforts of motivations and positive thinking. Also, there are many books for such things in the library, each volume 1, volume 2... There are many such and many quotations are available online, but the changes have not happened much, all the problems remain the same. No matter how many opinions and quotations are added, they will not be of much use. Why do you want to be negative on one side and positive on the other side? If we increase the problem little by little and solve it little by little, then we will feel like we have struggled as much as we have achieved. And we make loud noises. What is not in it is all a trick. In other words, we don't want to change. Have you heard about this positive thinking and motivation since childhood, and have you tried and got bored? Rather than practicing and memorizing all of them. It is very easy to work. When you start trying to be positive, the negativity increases in the back end.

We lose the naturalness of our mind with some meaningless things. When the work starts, there is a small movement in it. If you can identify some more, motivation, many more things are hidden, endless importance, and many more. The mind has to fulfill its meaning, but whatever it does is futile. Wanting security is what makes you unsecured. Everyone used to say this to everyone from childhood, but not everyone was able to do it, but for those who did, it was not a reason.

Topic-2: When the problem is serious, no prophecies, no philosophies make sense. Then motivation will not work. Then the problem should be solved immediately. It is important to understand the problem seriously. All other things, when they are empty. The mind has to be satisfied with it, until then whatever is done is of no use.

Topic-3: Who wants to be positive? Who is negative? Does what is negative want to be positive? Or are the two different? Why do you want to be like that? If a negative wants to be positive, will it become positive? If indeed it is so wonderful!. Sometimes we don't understand why we fall into the stream and get washed away!. Those who told us from childhood did the same and we are doing the same. I know that it will be of some use, that's why I am doing something. Never wondered why or how. While thinking that we don't want one, we get stuck in another. The same thing happened every now and then. Now it makes sense! How does negative still give life!?.. Oh! Want to stay? Not being!. Will it end if you want to have something? It will never change like this and if there is one there will be no other. To be clear, when something that has been meaningless for many years becomes meaningful, everything becomes positive. Or when a nonsensical formula makes sense, there becomes positive. There is no need to think that it should be separate again. The key is to understand something and then everything changes.

Topic-4: A person who is hungry should be given rice only, it is meaningless to preach the truth. Also, the mind needs to be satisfied and understood, whatever it does, it will be in vain. Sometimes, no matter how many efforts you make, it goes in a different direction, but you don't get what you want. If we don't understand or don't know some things, we give new names to existing things and spend time with them and think it is different. Example: Forming some thoughts and naming them as love. We do not even know that it is not. Understanding something naturally is different. But trying to think and understand about one thing is different, it goes in different direction. We strive for what is not in us, all those efforts are born from what is not, they change what is not yet, and yet they support what is not and change what is not yet but cannot bring something new. We want to be good because we have evil in us. Being is different from wanting to be. Now our efforts will start from that evil. No matter how many different names are given after transformation, it will not make much difference. Bad did not become good. We have negative in us so we want to be positive. There is no point in negative becoming positive and the two are not in the same place. If one is removed along with the roots, another will come and join. The same is true of many other things.

Topic-5: To put it simply about the motivation that we think sometimes.. It is as if we separate ourselves from ourselves, put some touches on it and request or order ourselves to do something again from it. Motivation is wanting.. It means wanting, it's like being lazy!. If it is considered a Lazy, it is also a part of it that separates from it. That's lazy too! will be What touches are there, what for what, what is the use of requesting and ordering. If the house catches fire, it needs to be saved immediately. There it is. There the situation immediately makes sense and it is intelligent in complete action. There is no one who motivates. There is not much time. It doesn't matter if you have a lot of time.. It is good to do whatever you want to be motivated. Also for that it would be very good to include some quotations like songs collection.

Topic-6: Why do we always need motivation? Why should we always be motivated? I don't understand why we are accepting all this without thinking about the direct problem without working directly?. They are all a trap, and they can become an addiction. From the moment efforts for positive thinking and motivation are started, negative ones also come to life and grow. That's why motivation and positive thinking are needed again. It repeats continuously. Who is not active? Who should be motivating whom? Isn't it all us.. Why all that?. No one likes to talk about the total disappearance of the problem, but if the problem is increased many times and reduced little by little, they like it better, it is all a part of motivation. Example: We don't think it is important to solve the problem but it is very important to make tools to solve the problem. There is only one problem, but we have created a hundred kinds of tools to solve that one problem. We are still making the same. Now those tools are too many and that's why we are increasing the problems a hundred times. But we have forgotten how to use those tools. If a small part of the energy used for unnecessary things is used for the problem, the problem will be removed easily. Once a problem occurs, attempts to make it go away are much less likely than attempts to avoid it. Motivation positive thinking means increasing the problem. If you stop all that and think why there is negativity, it will start to decrease. Then whatever is there is positive.

Topic-7: How much exercise the body needs! The brain also needs exercise. The brain is made the way it is trained. Adding different kinds of desires, feelings, emotions.. and creating unresolved problems becomes very heavy. Knowing that, we should not be a burden to the brain in confusion, stop learning new things, stop practicing. But in some things, knowledge, intelligence makes the brain work very actively, easily. Anything else makes sense very easily. It is as if there is no problem if a thing is understood easily. Also, if you increase awareness in all matters, life will become very easy. Example. A project work or a subject seems like a big problem in the beginning. If it starts learning and comes to the end, that big problem becomes very small. Also, learning things and increasing awareness makes the brain easier. But adding different kinds of desires, feelings, emotions to the same task... and creating hopeless problems becomes very heavy for the brain. Thought never solves the problems thought creates. That's why we need to know what is necessary and what is not necessary. The brain has a lot of power but we don't use even ten percent of our entire life.

Topic-8: Positive thinking and negative thinking. As a child, it was natural! What happened next? You are talking like this.. How it used to be, how it has become is very great. However, the problem you face is different from what you have thought before.

What you think is related to the problem you get?. Thinking ahead is not a suit for the upcoming new problem, it should be thought of when the problem arises. I don't know all that. Positive means to handle any situation! How can it be known in advance..?

8

Competition & Comparison

We think less and more to ourselves, but whose lives are theirs, whose problems are theirs. Cycle is awesome Airplane is awesome. What is the value of what is the use of what is what, there is no comparison. The reason we are in the situation we are in may be the environment we grew up in, the opportunities that came our way, the choices we made. Everyone's problems are the same wherever they go in the world. Life is much bigger than what we think and all the little things in it. Work plan, learning, practice, intelligence, talent are different. We want something and think that it is something else, but it is a lie that something will happen only because of thought, it will eventually become what it will be. What is now is also something. The world needs people who sell vegetables and people who make computers. And everyone needs all kinds of people. The world cannot go on without anyone.

Topic-2: Once in this competitive world it becomes difficult to survive without competition.. and there is nothing but tears.

But in a way we are very lucky to be in the competition. Because if we are in competition, we have opportunities! It means that we are working on something.. but we still don't know how to move forward. If we don't have any real competition, it means that we are empty. Actually, if you don't go on the road, there won't be any traffic! At least you should be very happy to be in some kind of traffic. Now the problem is how to handle that traffic? Everyone knows that you have reached this stage even if you worked very hard. What is the problem? Our talent and energy are not enough for the current situation. It is very easy for anyone to work but most of the time due to mental stress the mind is not working properly. In one stage, the mind becomes blank as the pressure increases while being well conditioned. The reason for that is that we take everything to heart and keep adding weight, it becomes an unbearable burden. Apart from that, if you treat it like a different experience, like a game, without taking everything to heart, it will be a lot of relief. There are very few people who work harder in any field. If we are included in it, there is less competition. And the deeper we go with our talent, the less the competition. One should always know how to do less work and more output, that is what smart work means. There is no game without an opponent. You have to decide whether you want to be in the game or not.

Topic-3: You are suffering a lot in comparison! But in relation to that, what special talent do you have?, have you ever thought about what other skills you have? Think about them first. If it comes naturally to others then why the pain? It is not what they have achieved! As if what they have achieved is not theirs! If they really work hard, respect their hard work and the same will apply to you later.

Topic-4: Everyone who wins says to get up in the morning, do yoga. But they also know that those are not the reasons for them to win. Everyone could be so great if it were really the same reasons. Why do all that? What are the real greats?.. Now the problem is not the same? Whose role is theirs, that's why everyone is great! There are many types of people in the world who are doing their jobs in many different ways and are very satisfied, so the world is very calm, otherwise it would be very turbulent. We should really salute all of them. What is your problem if they keep doing what they want? It's all about you seeing more and less, isn't it? This is one of the problems they have. What work is great? What do you say? Depending on the talent and skills, their level and their priority will change. If you want to do something, you have to plan and do it. What can we say about what is great? Is farming great? Is business great? What can we say.. Every work is great!. Think for a moment how the world is running.. is it running because of you?. Many people are indirectly the reason why we are here. The world needs everyone. They want a king, they want a pawn, that's why everyone is great. Sometimes no matter how many skills you have, opportunities do not come. What's the use when there are no opportunities. That's why let's give value to everyone, let's do what is right for them..

9

Energy Loss due to Conflict & Unnecessary things

We naturally have the power to face certain problems when needed but we make ourselves lose that power. Problems are outside.. Time will decide when some of them will be solved but they are imprinted in the mind and they try to change them in the mind but not outside, the situation outside remains the same, but the efforts are done in the mind.. They become burdensome and the energy decreases.

Topic-2: Life is too short, make it even shorter with unnecessary things. There is a lot of history that we don't know. Because history has been born for several million years. Ten more births are not enough to know all that. Sometimes we don't think it's important to face the problem head on. We are looking for the reasons and having big discussions about them and giving suggestions. Spending time with unnecessary things instead of doing what should be done. Don't try to know what talent we have to survive. Eg: Everything burns with fire, instead of trying to put it out, we look for reasons. When and where was the fire born for the first time, how did the first human beings make the fire, and in what era was it invented? Let's think about such things. We don't learn how to fight when we have to fight. We think about when the first war was fought, who fought it, what weapon was used first time, etc. Spending time with unnecessary things instead of doing what should be done. After the damage is done, whatever is done will not be of much use. Because history is not relevant to the situation we are in now, they have happened and gone. Now, it is important to know what and how to do it. You have a vehicle in your hand, you have to go far, knowing how to drive the vehicle is enough. Other things are not necessary then.

Topic-3: That is to say.. some problems repeat like this and remain elusive. Whether we know it or not, we accept it and experience it. I don't want to now. If you strongly dislike something, it will start again. Example: From now on I think that I should not be afraid, but invitation goes to fear. That means we invite fear again without knowing it. Then they are made like two sides of a coin. If you don't want one, another one will be added in the back end. And from now on, as I want to be good, the invitation goes to evil. Same will repeat. This is a reason for conflict. As long as a purposeful effort is made it will remain so. To put it more clearly, we have to remember what we want to forget. That's why forgetting doesn't happen as long as efforts are made. Because that effort is about forgetting it. The problem here is to yearn to be different without understanding it clearly. The invitation will go when you don't want it and it will repeat as well. If you understand what is there and realize the truth, it will be clear, whatever is there will come and reach.

Topic-4: Many problems have been stored in us and new ones are also being stored regularly. Quotations found outside, four good words, meditation, sympathy, good feeding for them. They still want something new. That is why we are still searching for good fodder for them. When you find good quotations, you will find relief and satisfaction, but there is no end to them. Thinking about how to get rid of all that again, I think the same realization.

Topic-5: Past: When the haunting memories of the past pile up and become an unbearable burden. Starting something new and being new becomes very difficult. So, to let go of the past, remember some things and prepare a list and if you want to let go, it's like you are still adding touches to the past! Remembering what you want to forget and trying to forget, how can you forget? The past cannot be changed, there is no chance to change the past, but if efforts are made in the mind, it will happen, but because of those efforts, it will repeat again. Observing everything that happens as it is, one gets an understanding of it, then whatever is needed becomes easy, there is no problem with it. Example. There is no problem because there is subject and knowledge, they do not create any quarrel, they are not a burden at all.

Topic-6: How much are we If you want to be strong and positive, negative will be created as strong in its back end. Then there is a conflict between the two. If there is a contradiction, it means that it is not positive. When you are really positive, you don't even know you are positive. There is no such focus.

10

Confusion

We know how to solve many problems easily. But we don't want to solve it so easily. Don't solve it so easily. Because there is no such thing as having achieved something or working hard. That's why it's a little bit longer and a little bit stretched. We are the ones who accept and feed the problem, we are the ones who look for solutions elsewhere. Separation, escaping is a trick. After knowing that there is no use in looking elsewhere for solutions, turning somewhere, asking someone, we will finally understand ourselves. Some prefer to remain the same.

Topic-2: It is good when there is no problem.. because it was done correctly and there was no problem. Then we don't need to think about why it is so. But when you accidentally fall into a problem, it takes a lot of time to know how to do it correctly and to get out of that problem. Some take life. No matter where you turn, no matter how much anyone says, whatever you do will be in vain. No one can say how to make meaning. Ultimately we have to understand ourselves.

Also, while doing some tasks in particular, the problem starts with a small undetectable reason and later becomes the main one. Then the reasons are not so easy to understand and it becomes very difficult to get out of it.

Topic-3: In any case, the concept is clearly defined, but many paths are visible. It is very easy, simplify the thoughts and don't strain so much. Then even if one path is closed, many more paths will appear. But when the concept doesn't make sense, there are forced efforts. Even a path can become very difficult. It does not mean what we are doing. Something else is wanted but nothing happens. In the absence of output, no matter how much work is done, it comes down to what is not. And all time becomes waste and hell. There are many things that we have created ourselves. Especially in the matter of children, if we can do it without any confusion, it will be a good week for them. If the mind is cool and calm, work will be done speedily without mistakes. This is possible only when the mind is natural. But in hurrying to do something, many factors are involved and there are many confusions in it, work does not go well. If you observe and understand the meaning of each and every thought, space will be created in the mind, it will become powerful and it will start coming closer to naturalness.

Topic-4: Following special methods and special formulas seems good at first.. but as days pass by they become very difficult, headache and very boring. Apart from that, if all of them can be well understood, simplified and inbuilt in daily activities, there is nothing better than that. Then there will be no separate thinking, no separate principles and very peaceful

Topic-5: Thinking with the intention of getting out of the problem is like deviating from it! It doesn't make sense and then leads to escape. Still growing never goes away. Apart from that, if you start thinking about the problem seriously, the problem becomes very small and goes away.

Topic-6: The more we imagine the work we want to do, the more we boast about it!.. the harder it becomes to reach that goal. We have created that gap. We create such a gap especially in children. That becomes difficult for them.

Topic-7: Once in a while we will be in confusion, there will be no clarity where we are, we will be in confusion. Example: Himalayas painting on paper is only an indication that it is not really Himalayas. The rest will come later. But here we are. Being here and still having the same opinion, thinking the same thing, I feel like I am reaching and achieving. But if the existing state does not make sense, that something cannot happen.

Topic-8: Psychologically, who accepts and experiences problems? Later, being separated from them.. Who makes efforts to go away?. It's all a Trick & Endless process.

Topic-9: After going back and forth about a matter in many places and making a decision thinking that one is best... then when you know that something else is best and you are not in a position to change what you think is best.. the pain is not normal. Sometimes some do not understand beforehand.

Topic-10: The world will not stop because you have a problem now.. Problems are not only for you but for everyone. Life is not only for you but for everyone.

Topic-11: A few hundreds of thousands of thoughts are coming every day but it doesn't mean where they connect in life?..

11

Condition

Physical conditioning is absolutely necessary to achieve anything. Making a work plan according to the calendar is hard work according to the time.. all that is physical.. it has to be. But no mental condition is required. Mind can work well only if it is very free. Sometimes we mentally think later but later is a lie. The situation may be the same later. Without starting work...without spending some time in work, new ideas will not come and there will be no creativity. There is nothing but growing ideas. Escaping exists as long as we expect that we have other options. But work starts when we understand that we have no other work but this work. As long as you are on the bank of a river, there are various thoughts, but if you go down into the river, you have to walk. When a work is started and done continuously, some new techniques are learned in that work.. That is what creativity is. Then everything will make sense.

Topic-2: Bringing internal discipline through external discipline is a lie. External is physical activity.. What changes happen in the mind with it?. Internal discipline comes from understanding. It doesn't work with time. A thing does not mean something over a period of time or changes over a period of time. All followers try to bring internal discipline through external discipline but it is never possible. That's why very few people in the world become creators, and all others become their followers. They copy everything and practice the same. By doing that, they are under the illusion that one day they will become great. Practice is repeated it becomes mechanical.. There is no creativity and growth in it. That's why they remain the same no matter how many years. Hence, all those who want to become, cannot become. It can be possible when you understand what is there well, leave it and start with new ideas on your own.. What it means will be different, and it will be experiential.. They will know that. They themselves become creators. They have no replacement. Proof of that.. If you look at all the fields. They should know whether to be a follower or a creator. It is not about social media follow but only about profession.

Topic-3: Whatever we feel about ourselves and create some things, they prevent us from working freely. In some things, positive or negative, we create some things and they lock us. But the work has nothing to do with those feelings. We are caught in the net we weave. The events that happen in real life have nothing to do with what we gather in our mind.

Topic-4: To solve the problem, to listen to moral stories, there is no relationship. No matter how many ethical stories you hear, how many quotations you put, still waiting for new ones. It becomes like an addiction. As long as there are listeners, there will be tellers. Telling stories may be their profession, but even if they listen to all of them, miracles in the world will not happen.

Why are all the conditions the same? We need to know what is going on. Who will identify that we are in problem? Who will collect moral stories so that they all go away? There are people who have wasted many years for something like this, in confusion. No matter how much moral stories are fed to them while nurturing side problems, their hunger will not be satisfied. Need a weapon to remove roots. We have to find it for ourselves. Anything makes sense to us easily. When it is like that, only time will decide when the next step will be, or there will be some things that we will correct immediately. But we want to separate from there and change there. Then the original problem remains. The problem does not come into being separate, and from there it is of no great use.

Topic-5: Making a work plan according to the calendar is different, it is physical, it has to be there. Mentally later is a lie. Later is going to be done later, later is going to change, and later is a word created for present satisfaction and the situation may be the same later. And if you sometimes want to do something but can't do it, then the reason may not make sense. But because of not being able to do that work, we find a hundred reasons against it, and if that work is waste, there is no use for it, if we create and do not do that work again, then we feel satisfaction.

Topic-6: It is different from collecting things and putting them together, looking for meaning in them and relying on them. It is different to know and understand moment by moment and move forward. Collecting and putting things together does not work well, intelligence and creativity do not increase. There is wisdom and creativity in moving forward by knowing and understanding moment by moment, there is growth and there is novelty, it is like a complete action movie.

Topic-7: The moments of hard work in the past are well remembered. With those memories, we want to work hard in the future as well. Those memories become an unbearable burden. The present is made without doing anything. Unknowingly worked hard in the past. Now that the experience has come, even more can be done. Life long is not enough for what was hard in the past. When memories become too heavy to carry, it becomes difficult to start a new one. We want to face the future with the past but it doesn't let the work go smoothly.

Topic-8: The deficit created during the period of control and adjustment will be compensated many times later. But understanding is different, it is always the same.

Topic-9: If you want to get fame or good results or anything else, there is no concentration on the work and there is no output. But work, for work, doing is one thing, if it can be identified, all the same will be set. While doing some things, we cannot avoid correcting some things that seem correct. We do it for internal satisfaction. If you have such a view..even in the profession, perfection will come in the work and then it will become like a passion. It is work, doing it for work. There are no other expectations in it.. Work is not done for the sake of anything. Especially for children, if this can be made aware and not for the meaningless future.. If they realize that such a view exists, their creativity will be set automatically. Sometimes the employer is not correct or the circumstances are not good, we do not do the work properly, we spoil our career and if we change our character, we will not be able to work for anything later. If our expectations and some circumstances do not influence and change what we do, it will be different.

Topic-10: Always wanting something gives good satisfaction. But that is not true. Being is the only truth. Wanting is different. Being is different.

Topic-11: It's not over.. it actually just started. Every movement is new but the mind is there making them old and accumulating them all. If you fall into the entanglements of memories, you will not reach the flow of life.

Topic-12: Death is an end to us, to our problems... It may be a great loss to us but it is only a small movement to creation. Every move is a new beginning. Experience is infinite, but sensations bring past memories into what is known, but nothing ceases.

Topic-13: Some of the memories that were once created are still haunting. Now they have become the yardstick for everything done. Anything done is compared as more or less. But everything is a different experience and new too.. the mind links them to the old and turns them into the old.

Topic-14: There is a problem in one part of the body and that pain makes all the other parts take rest, similarly a small disturbance in the mind removes all the mind and makes it take rest without allowing it to do any work. Also, whoever has a problem in the family, that family will be crippled. No matter how many such things come, it is very difficult to balance. And it's hard to make sure it doesn't come true because there are always going to be some mistakes.

CONDITION

Topic-15: Life is too short, there is so much to do.. Even the smallest things, if you make it difficult and feel like it's too hard!. The things that still need to be done pile up and it becomes really difficult.

Topic-16: Thought never solves the problems it creates because it is the creator and the solution is the same!. Without understanding the desires, changing the desired things and thinking the same growth? There is a difference between having a physical work plan and eating when you are hungry. But making psychologically insatiable desires is different. That's the problem. Small example: the scenario is very good in a photo but if we actually go to that place, we don't get the same feeling. That's where the two separate in the mind. Once in a while or in the case of some people, an image is created in the mind after hearing about a famous city somewhere. Even if you go to that city later, it may not be as expected. But the starting image in the mind remains the same. It's like you have to visit that city sometime. That means two different things are changing. This is just a small example to understand. The same happens in the case of unfulfilled desires. What is desired, even after it is done, seems not to be. That desire separates and grows, the things desired, no matter how much they change, remain the same. It is irrelevant to that. The whole world is no match for what a thought creates. This can also be a reason for injustices happening outside. Without understanding the desires, whatever is done will result in wrongdoing. It does not make much difference whether the desires are well developed, or without desires at all. Whether it is positive or negative, there is the same conflict in the mind and then it takes any form. It is important to understand desires rather than giving them up or increasing them.

Topic-17: The hatred you harbored against them is not theirs, it is a part of you. It destroys you but not them. In other words, the hatred you harbored against me is not mine, it is a part of you. It is a threat to you but not to me.

Topic-18: Analyzing purposefully will turn things in your favor but not really find the problem. And there is no knowing what is correct. Also, the world you understand is different, the world I understand is different. What makes sense to you doesn't make sense to me. Because your intentions are yours and my intentions are mine. We want to understand according to them. But there is one which has no connection with any motives, and it is different if it is meaning. We see everything with condition. But if it is not with that condition, it will be different.

Topic-19: When we are doing what we like, it doesn't feel difficult and we don't even know the time.. But in order to tell others how hard we are working, we make the work very difficult in our mind, and we feel like it is very hard.. Then it becomes very difficult. We stay with the same memories.. Later we forget that the work is easy for us.

Topic-20: If some problems stay with you for a long time, then that problem is yours, not the problems. It means that you are feeding them. Well, if you like it that much, who can deny it?.. Send an invitation even to the forgotten problems and start anew, it's your choice.

Topic-21: We are very happy if a very difficult task that we want

CONDITION

to do becomes easy without our knowledge. Actual life is also the same, but life is not so good if we don't know it, if we make everything a problem and feel like it is very difficult.. it feels like life.

Topic-22: Life is somehow not eternal so eternity is sought in later generations.

12

Depression

In creation, no living being commits suicide except man. Such is the case with a man of great intellectual power. It takes a lot of energy, determination and courage to do that. But if all of them are used to deal with the problem, the problem will be solved easily, but it doesn't happen? They know what they are doing is wrong but it does not stop happening. Energy abilities should be used as they are meant to be used, if they are misused they will destroy us. The real problem has nothing to do with dying. As the outsiders understand that what they are doing is wrong, they also understand it, so they commit suicide when no one else comes near and there is no one. Most of us are the ones who come and go until the end of our lives. Due to the conflict created in the mind, we become our enemy. We ourselves raise high expectations in some things or create over depression. All that is related only to us. External situation has no link to what happens inside. Some link every situation to death. Attempts to intimidate once in a while are also truly trans formative. In some cases what appears on the outside is not true. All their reputations and external pretensions cannot touch the inner turmoil. They are the ones who say that someone should be like this! If it was that easy, everyone would be fine. But no one can answer what is inside. We have to decide for ourselves. Many say that you have to conquer the mind.. You have to know yourself, but it is not that easy. For every situation that happens outside, an image is automatically created in us through our own thoughts. Whatever it is, it is only related to us, it is what we have created, the external situation may not be suitable for it. In that case, the image that we have created will be damaged and then an unbearable situation will occur. Understanding each situation and doing what is correct is different. Over-liking is over-dependence. That's different. That's cheating.

Topic-2: The words heard and said well from childhood "must work hard, must be persistent, must have concentration, creativity... must achieve something... must be great". Due to such things, the pressure increases and it becomes important to think about the future and not work properly. We will come to the stage where we would like everything to happen without working, and we will continue to try in that way. All that is conditioned without our knowledge. There is no use in forcing will and practice. Some can be reverse without meaning and even become lazy. Those who say, we still do not understand how to learn and understand what is there. All this is based on what happened in some people's lives, some words were used depending on what they did....the reason for them could be anything else. These words are not the reason. We want to hold the words and work through them?...and we want to go to work with the words but these words have nothing to do with the work being done. We are losing the naturalness of our brain. Direct doesn't need these words to work, something else has to be found. Stress is emotionally draining.

Topic-3: When dreams and thoughts about the future deviate from the present situation and prevent work from progressing, the same thing happens later!. What else is there to think big and achieve? That's why you should be alert and pay attention.

Topic-4: About your pain, your sorrow, your difficulty... no one cares so much, it doesn't matter so much. Everything related to you seems very small and very lite to them... But why do you hang on to them when they seem very lite and very small to them?. Still trying to say something but what is so special about it? I do not understand! Leave everything and be calm. Usually we think too much about ourselves, and if there are still listeners, we start new ones, some of which have no end. That makes sense.

Topic-5: Some children also find it difficult to be more intelligent. When they have negative thoughts, they use all their intelligence on them and go far. It is very difficult to get them from there. They go as deep as they have intelligence, so getting out becomes equally difficult.

Topic-6: Words do not hurt anyone but the intention behind the words hurts a lot. Some people are under the illusion that their intentions are not meaningful to others.

13

Freedom

The mind always desires freedom, but that desire itself deprives it of freedom. Truth is understood only when there is freedom. Many organizations make a big fuss about this and try hard to tell. But those organizations are conditioning without freedom. The organization itself is the condition. And what is there to know about freedom and truth? They don't know that either. On the one hand we are conditioned and on the other hand we strive for freedom. In other words, the mind is still free, but the desire for security destroys freedom.

Topic-2: Why are you struggling and carrying everything to the end? Death somehow wipes it all out. That's why life will be easy if you leave the unnecessary garbage now. The weights we carry physically are temporary, we get relief when we leave them, but some psychologically, we carry them for many years without knowing, they become a burden that we cannot bear.

Topic-3: If the mind is free, it will be different, there is no giving up, it will be as it is, meaning, the way of thinking will be different. Even if you go to a beautiful place with a conditioned mind, you will not be happy. If the same mind is free, the grass will also be very good. And so is life. Because we are conditioned like that, we do not recognize other people as human beings, we also appear like that to other people. What is the problem if a man is recognized as a man? As a child, there was nothing, then the mind was very free and intelligent, whatever was done was free. Later everything changed and now even those who cry have to cry as an engineer. At the end of life, if you think that some small thing has meaning and everything is missed, nothing will come back. But if some things make sense and an understanding of life comes, it will be different. If you understand what is not first, then you will know that other state. But if you try to do it again, the same will repeat itself.

Topic-4: Anger is a natural characteristic of every living being to protect itself. Anger is very powerful. It plays a major role in our life as well as necessity. It is used for good and it is used for destruction. Physically, when some situations slip out of hand, in an attempt to control the situation, and in an attempt to put the evil in a good direction, Parents, Teachers come in an attempt to put the children in regular training. It's all physical.. it comes and goes automatically, no problem. But it has been known for many years that it has been made psychologically for self-interest. It is mixed with grudge, jealousy, hatred and desire and leads to destruction. Makes you without peace of mind and does not go away easily. Without fully understanding some things, no matter how much effort you make, even going to the Himalayas will not be of much use.

Topic-5: Freedom does not mean giving up all control and being independent of anything. Not having favorites yet. It is about making sense of the present life. Only human beings are born with different types of emotions.. Anger, Jealousy, Urgency, Fear, Sadness, Frustration, Depression, Guilt, Pain, Desire, Pain, Disgust, Surprise, Love, Laughter, Admiration, Wave, Happiness, Joy.. There are many. Those who told us said that some of it should be given up and some should be held. Is that really possible!?. Why give up what comes naturally? How to give up? It doesn't make sense. Knowing that truth makes sense if it is free. But how is it freedom to hold some and let some go? It is not freedom to give up everything. It will be an escape. But let us know a little about what freedom is. An emotion comes and goes depending on a situation in everyone's life. There is no need to give up anything. Can't really do that, if it does it will do the same thing indirectly. If so, what is the problem? But what can we do? Can we stop the emotions between a mother and child? Can we stop the emotions between wife and husband? Waste of effort, no use. Look into compassion, look into anger and understand what the purpose is, go to work and see what is beautiful in it, see the depth of a song, see the love of a mother and children, see the love of a father, see the love of a husband, see the love of a wife, see the love of an elder brother, see the love of a sister. See the difficulty of the man who sweeps the road, see the difficulty of the man who lifts the stones, see the ebb and flow of everyone, go into the painting and see its beauty, see the sun, go into the subject depth and see, listen to the pain of others and see that pain inside.. while looking deeply. You will know something beautiful. When you understand what depth is instead of escape, it becomes free. But if you accumulate all of them, it becomes a condition again. What is still to be done is a long journey, do not stop anywhere, be like mercury and do not cling to anything. Freedom means being one with all. not like that some want, some don't want. When they are understood it becomes freedom. When we think about all this, we feel how small we are living life. It seems that we are living on the surface. In other words, we are the world and the world is us. In some sense, once the light is on, it stays the same. Nothing extinguished it. It is said that life is great but how can it be?, it only makes sense if the mind is free.

Topic-6: Have you ever noticed what is happening outside but always with you!. Look at the outside world. All great intellectuals know yourself.. That's it!. If you want to know yourself quickly, you need to know other things too! But that doesn't mean you have to stay with yourself for the rest of your life. Have you ever seen the rising sun? Nothing! Not as you think. It is not part of the work of gathering for that purpose because someone has said that doing so will bring good. Have you ever really felt it? Are you looking without any purpose? Have you ever seen yourself free from the entanglements you have made? Also, in terms of work, it is clearly not free, so it does not make much sense. All that is known when the mind is free. What is not clearly understood by mind as a condition.

Topic-7: To tell a lie.. you have to think a lot, plan, there is no guarantee that you will remember the same later, you have to make a lot of efforts to remember the same, and you have to suffer a lot. But telling the truth doesn't require much thought and effort. You know what is better! I don't have that much patience. A lie can be chosen and still be changed in any way but the truth cannot be chosen, it cannot be changed, it is what it is.

Topic-8: No problem is permanent.. Life is not permanent. Everything that started has to end! As if there is no more problem!

Topic-9: We have an image about ourselves and from that we observe all things and try to understand according to it.. but nothing comes to clarity with it. How many thoughts about ourselves are decreasing?, external things also start to make sense with clarity..

14

Missing Present

Now we are something That's who we are. There are no unexpected miracles. What we know is what happens day by day, and that is what we need to make a miracle.

Topic-2: Small thoughts make us miss a wonderful person inside us, if we can't bring out that person, there will be no more miracles.

Topic-3: Every movement in life is very important..everything should be experienced. It is not available anywhere in the market. Especially the experience related to ourselves is not found anywhere in the world. Even if you make a thousand plans, it is not natural, but that plan is also a part of it! Life is an endless experience from starting to end.. But what you don't want, what you want, what you want, all are parts of it! But due to some confusions, separations are created and there is always conflict.. nothing makes sense. Anything, if its value is meaningful, is mind calm. When we are in one stage we think about another stage. It feels good even before going to the next stage. But do not experience it in that time. Example: Children don't understand how good school life is. Even what we have before us now will not come later. I think so later too. Wanting to be always separates what is. To be clear, there is no tomorrow. There is really nothing before us except to see tomorrow in forward thinking. If you want to see tomorrow, you have to wait until tomorrow. Only thoughts about tomorrow are not real. It does not mean that there is no future here, whatever we thought before, it will be different until it comes to reality. But in that time, the present is being missed. It means that there is no link between what is thought before and what happens later. Why do you think so? According to the calendar, planning work, learning, practicing, intelligence and talent are different.

Topic-4: Experience is infinite but the feeling is past memories, taking in the known, that is me. Also we are trying to conduct all our activities from there. We try everything with I, with thought, but a lot happens without thought. The same is done with direct intelligence. When you are hungry, you know it automatically, not with thought. Break suddenly while driving, not with thought. Then there will not be much time, it will be done directly with intelligence. There are many. Birds are very clever at making nests. And some living beings show great intelligence, but they do not have so much thinking power, which is all done by intelligence. A lot happens regardless of thought. But we don't know. A lot of space is created in the mind if some things are really meaningful. There are no unnecessary thoughts. A few hours can be without any thought. Ideas come and go when they are needed.

Topic-5: Work plan, learning, practice, intelligence, talent are different. But between what we are and what we want, there are many thoughts going on. We think that we need something, without valuing what we have, without understanding it, and we think that it would be better if it were different. But it is false to think that something will happen only because it will eventually become what it will be. Life keeps the mind busy with meaningless things. Do not always be empty thinking about wanting something. Always wanted to be but not. We will miss what is still life. Want something and become something else. That's why we are reluctant, but the present is also something. The world needs vegetable sellers, computer makers, and everyone else. We need all kinds of people, and without them, the world cannot go on. Until we understand the reality of what we are not, we do not know some values and some problems are inevitable.

Topic-6: The scenario looks very good in a photo but if we actually go to that place we will not get the same feeling. Love seems very good in the movie but not so good in practical terms! Why? When something is seen from the outside, it is good, but when it is involved, why is that feeling missing?.. Something is missing in life! It seems.. something doesn't make sense. And now it's difficult, so we think school life was better when we were young. But then we did not experience that school life was so good and did not recognize it. Then thinking about the future.. or the problems that existed then may be there. The same will happen now. Now we think that the childhood life will not return. If we go a little further, we think that even the present life will not return. Always missing something, thinking about it later? It is a fact that what does not come back. Always full of problems and looking at the outside world from within, then nothing is recognized properly. But after a few days, if you look back, you will not see the problems of then, because they are not there now, but only our life that happened will be seen.. It would be better if it was now. Example: No matter how beautiful a place you go to with a conditioned mind, there is no happiness. If the same mind is free, the grass will also be very good. And so is life. There is always something more that we want, so we feel that what we have now is not ours. Example: When we intend to get out of the problem, we don't care what it is, but the problem is that life meets them, they are not separate. Problems are solved when they are solved. New ones will keep coming.. But whether there is a problem or not, this life is ours, every situation is ours, before it becomes meaningful, the life then will be over. Every movement in life is very important. Everything has to be experienced, not if you want it later. It is not available anywhere in the market. Especially the experience related to ourselves is not found anywhere in the world.

Topic-7: Unknowingly, our experience conditions us and prevents us from being in the present without freedom.. but life is a link to the present that changes moment to moment. Intellect and truth are the same, being in the present, in the form of all those who work, and are alive in the whole world. Should they be the occasional light in your life? Or to be the light that is always with you? You should know that.

Topic-8: Walking on the railway track is very good to see in the movie song but if we go and walk like that in real, it will not be that good and we will not get that feeling. The scenario looks very good in a photo but if we actually go to that place we will not get the same feeling. Love seems very good in the movie, but it is not so good in practical terms??.. Something is missing in life, something is not understood. And now it's difficult, so I think school life was good when I was a child, but I don't realize that it was so good then.. I don't know what thoughts about the future or what else there are. Then I realized it wasn't that much and now it feels amazing. Now I think that my childhood life will not come back.. If I go a little further, I think that my present life will also not come back. When do you think about missing something later?.. It is a fact that nothing comes back. We are always immersed in problems and see the outside world from within, but the reality is different. Being is different. Wanting to be is different. Wanting to be always separates what is. Many things are understood and some are unknown unless the mind is clear. Always full of problems and looking at the outside world then it does not recognize it properly. But if we look back, we will see our life that has happened, then the problems will not be visible. I think it was missed. That's why put problems aside now.

15

Trap

When we know that something is impossible, we fall into the trap of what is possible. A lot of stories are woven in favor of what is possible. If we do not do that, we will not feel satisfaction. Trap is the easy way and very comfortable. After a few days it will be understood that it is not correct and then we will be very disappointed. There will be damage that cannot be repaired. Now in another trap. That is being in various addictions. They can be bad or good... It can be various habits, it can be keeping four good words together, it can be meditation that some people practice. All of them are part of the trap. To put it more clearly, it is like escaping without understanding the situation. Some things are not so easy to understand. It is normal for us to always be immersed in something. But what actually happens is different from being in reality. If anything is accepted as it is and understood as it is, it will not be all there is.

Topic-2: Being compatible and adjusting is always cheating, it will be a blast once in a while. Being agreeable is different from understanding. Being suitable and adjusting creates a different negative in the mind. It becomes an unbearable burden for a few days and everything reverses. Being in favor is like accepting something that is not right! But understanding is not like that, it becomes clear as soon as it is understood, it does not carry any weight, the mind is calm and empty. If some things don't make sense then, they will make sense later, but some confusions keep going in a different direction.

Topic-3: Sadness: There is a tear in everyone's story, behind that tear hides a lot of pain. Death is a very painful thing for everyone. No matter how much it hurts, it is not going to change. Aside from that, we take everything to heart. If we get hurt in childhood, we still carry that pain. Some mistakes happen unintentionally and that pain haunts you like a shadow. Some cannot be left so easily. There is no chance to change some things that have happened, but if there are efforts in the mind to change, those efforts will double the pain again and again. As we grow up, looking at the surroundings, we are conditioned by setting up some measurements with various comparisons that we should be like this and that. It hurts to go against it. If you can observe and understand what is as it is, it will not exist. And we want to hide some pains to tell them to our loved ones and get relief little by little by telling them. But what they say, together with their suggestions, sympathies and old memories, recreates that pain and makes a new version in the mind... that means the pain has increased. Now another one has come to our pain, and then others will come. Sometimes I like being with them. We are constantly adding and recreating these things and treating them like our properties.

Topic-4: It seems to be nothing, it seems to be nothing, but it is all encompassing. Everything drives the same, occasionally showing its cosmic form. At first it does not affect any habitual mind. Later on it grows a lot of love. Later on, it is a bit difficult to convert it to the opposite of that favorite. Then everything that is disliked becomes its opposite. Unknowingly now, the favorite is made even stronger. Even its roots are made without meaning to where they go. It does not want to do anything but what it likes now. Doing what is correct and doing what is necessary is different. Whatever is done without removing any roots is a copy of it. Habits can be good or bad for us and cause conflict in the mind.

Topic-5: If we tell our problem, someone will easily give suggestions and solutions.. Change or not depends on what we understand. But that is not the real problem. How to tell other people when we don't know that we are in problem? There is no realization because of being in a trap. When you realize that it is a problem.. Then you tell other people. But who among us can bring that realization? That's the problem. Until we don't understand anything, whatever anyone says or does will only be outside side efforts and outside control. Then there is no relation between what is inside us and what is happening outside. Some things we don't know ourselves, that's why we don't know how to tell the children, it's only when they understand. Until then, outside controlling is done. External discipline comes through controlling but internal discipline comes through understanding. But when it comes to internal discipline, outside discipline is like a small blade of grass. Then the time sense also doesn't work that much it looks different. It has become possible for some. If we are always in some world or in some trap, if we do not fall into the stream and get swept away, we can improve to some extent if we try to understand. To know yourself is to understand that something is there, but if you want to know whether you will become something great or if you want to gain some benefit, it does not make sense. And it will become another problem in addition to the existing ones. If we really get to know ourselves, that will solve all problems.

Topic-6: To know thyself is not to discover thyself. Life is over before it makes sense that it is different. It is normal for us to change something in our favor. Over the years, in trying to find ourselves, everything else has been missed. What's in it? Better wake up now.

16

Growth

The whole world is surrounded by energy in various forms.. How to get it depends on your talent.

Topic-2: You know you have a goal... but when you don't have a daily base target, that goal remains a dream.

Topic-3: Studies, software, problems in life.. anything else.. we have to rise to their level and understand them, but if they want to come down to our level, it will drag a great mountain into the valley, then it will lose its greatness and our growth will also stop there.

Topic-4: All problems can never be solved at once. Even if we have enough power to face all the problems right now, all the problems will not come now. Problems will come after looking at time. When you are strong, nothing seems to be a problem, when you are weak, everything becomes a problem.. It can be physical or psychological.

Topic-5: Intelligence comes and grows by understanding and thinking about existing situations. But it is not related to a particular age group, or to a system, or to some people, or to the generation of grandparents, or to famous people.

Topic-6: Everyone has energy, talent and intelligence, but if they don't know how to balance them, they will not be of much use. Example: A volleyball, football players can break the ball, There may be power but doing so is not winning. When you learn how to play the game and practice well, everything balances automatically. The same happens in other matters as well.

Topic-7: Every problem has it's own roots. If you cut the problem it will come again. If you remove the roots it will come to an end.

Topic-8: Sometimes one does not know the way to face the enemy but the same enemy indirectly shows the way to face himself. This world shows many paths if you have to put your mind to it. Example: In games, our opponent shows us the way without our knowledge.

Topic-9: When the path is full of fog, the path is not clear! Likewise, thoughts like fog also make the goal not clear. Nothing can be done until the goal is clear. As long as something is not meaning, so are many ideas, and if meaning, they are not all. You have to do a lot of groundwork for anything, then the same meaning will come and the same clarity will come. That's what life is all about.

Topic-10: The happiness of thinking is only until then. Not always. For it to always be there, one should stop mentally lighting small lamps, then a light like a sun will appear beyond thought which will always make one happy and solve all problems.

Topic-11: Our quality, our talent.. will make us famous. But later in confusion, thinking about that name and searching for that name, we destroy that quality and that talent.

Topic-12: If we notice that there are any minor mental problems in the children, we should try to eliminate them without their knowledge. If we make them aware of the problems that we do not know or not with our intelligence and reprimand them, they will not be fixed. And the problem becomes so strong that they don't know how to get out. Then we need to support more. No problem is permanent.

Topic-13: Be very careful when the problem is too hidden to be discovered. Hopes and confidences are useless. Unknowingly, they get confused and try different things. But don't do what you have to do. And the original problem remains the same. It is a lie that if you do this then that will happen and if you do that then this will happen. It's all about escaping. Why do that? Whatever can be done according to the need. A fact is meaningless if there is a prior intention. Once the damage is done, realize is of no use.

Topic-14: When there are efforts, do not stay at work. When engrossed in work, there is no effort. Listening does not exist as long as efforts are made to hear something particular. Meditation does not exist as long as efforts are made for meditation. Efforts always separate work. If the mind is calm, everything happens automatically, but being calm is a very difficult task.

When one is very serious about a work, there is no scope for efforts, one has to work directly. Efforts always separate direct work. As long as efforts are made we are not clear Energy abilities are not properly utilized Work does not go well Direct work without efforts is different. Practicing feels like physical effort.. but physical effort is not separate work, it is all a part of work. Psychological efforts separate us from work and they are not necessary.

Topic-15: Things that are understood and learned through experience do not make sense if we think normally and cannot be understood that much. That's why it's important to work. Some are set automatically by working. But nothing happens automatically by just thinking. Actually we are not able to perform as well as we want to. What we do has nothing to do with what we want. So leave some unnecessary things. It is better to understand what is possible for us and do the same. Then the status quo starts changing.

Topic-16: If you work without expecting the result, the result will be good.. is another kind of expectation. Do you think that it does not make sense if it confuses something?... When some intentions do not make sense, it does the same in some form. Even if we don't want to do some work, we collect some and change here and there and get satisfied. People who really work don't care about all that, they don't have much time, they know the result of their work. Example: If time is set as 10 minuts fast then we know indirectly so we use that time also. What is the use of it? We want the same in some form and not in confusion. All of that is important to understand. When it makes sense, it is on the right path.

Topic-17: Charity is not only about giving money.. but also about doing something to help. This world has given us so much. We don't know what form, where and how we got help from this world, it's all charity. Through nature, through parents, through family members, through the love of elders at home, through online, through society, through literature, through friends, and we get inspired by seeing someone else... We get what we want in one form or another. All that is charity. History repeats itself as the help received in one form is returned in another form. Charity is not only about giving money, we can help in different ways.. Example: We can share our knowledge, we can give a solution to a problem that has been bothering someone for many years, we can redirect a cow that has lost its way, we can tell a new person if they ask for an address, we can cross an old man on the road, anything that is hungry. You can help animals in any way you want... If you think about it, there are many things you can do.

Topic-18: We don't have health principles and tips as you think!. How do we know if it is suitable for you? They should know what is correct for them and protect their health. Sometimes some may not be in our hands. But at least we can't try to save what we have in our hands. Let's do exercise, let's follow some principles, we postpone the day to tomorrow, but tomorrow is a lie. We give a lot of advice to other people without doing anything but they know a lot. However, knowing something alone is not enough. If you do what you can, what is the problem? Health is a blessing.

Topic-19: Analysis is not the way...we analyze to eliminate fear, but analysis reinforces fear and feeds fear. Also analysis is increasing the problem in the relationship. Anything done without understanding is useless.

Topic-20: Millions of hardships for the stomach. When will these difficulties end? But in a way it can be said that it will never end, because as long as there is life, there will be difficulties. At times, unable to cope with these problems, one wants to leave everything and run away. Or something else needs to be done. But can you find a more wonderful life if you give it all up? Can't find it. There are problems with comparing too much. We think that we are the only ones who are having a hard time and others are not having any difficulties. Others seem to have a better life. But everyone is in the same situation. Everyone's problems are their own. Different people have different problems. Profession wise and position wise may be different but life is same for all. Not everyone can be a king. Not everyone can be a soldier. The world needs everyone, it needs people who make computers, it needs people who sell vegetables. These problems are due to discrimination of less as more. Humans have different difficulties. I want to leave everything and die. But there is one in between to let go, to die. Leave everything psychologically and don't give up anything physically. Look at everything as a game and don't take anything to heart. Then it will be calm.

Topic-21: It is a lie that all those who tell Purana are truthful and only they know the truth. Truth is the same for all who have to know it.

Topic-22: But they have the fire for that work, so they are able to work without knowing the time. Why do you care about them? And don't you want to know what work you have fire in!?.

Topic-23: In a way.. our life is not ours it is also our next generations!. Because the path we take, the path we walk will be a guide for generations to come.

Topic-24: It's okay to want to see everything. And when are you going to make other people want to be like you after seeing what you have done?

Topic-25: When some good opportunities are left unrecognized and the existing opportunities are not used properly.. all those situations become enemies and take revenge. And some memories haunt like shadows. All of them are present in everyone's life but if we do not try to correct them even if we get out of them, the same situation will continue.

Topic-26: We know that the way the brain works, the intelligence that the brain exhibits is amazing, we know that it works automatically in some things. We have an idea about it. Because it is so great, we are under the illusion that we can do miracles without working hard, and we will become something else. We also know that we have deceived ourselves many times since childhood. We also know that something is not without hard work, but we will be in some kind of dream.. because it creates those dreams automatically as well. If it is working, it is not serious. As if in some world, we are doing something because we have to do it. Eg. Some have ten years of experience and remain the same. Some people have one month experience but they are same as ten years old people.. means their way of working is different. The brain creates many miracles, and it deceives us just as wonderfully. When any input is not correct, the output is also not correct. What is fed is what is made. Keeping an eye on them, it is better to wake up and be a little serious

Topic-27: Future is useless if it is not according to schedule but in imagination, it will remain as it is.. that will be future.

Topic-27: The fact that we have more personal problems does not reduce the problems in our work. The problems we face at work have nothing to do with our personal problems. That's all we think.. There is no such thing. No matter how difficult it is, there is no excuse. Every situation is ours and we have to face it ourselves.

Topic-28: There is a lot of pain in every work but when we have a passion in that work, the pain is not so much, it is all like it. And you should know why that passion is not there..

Topic-29: When an opportunity is in our hands, we can do something as long as that opportunity is in our hands.. How much quality to do and how to shape it is all in our hands. Once left, there is no going back, nothing can be done again, it remains the same for life. That is why it is better to try to do everything perfectly.

Topic-30: If we want to start a new work, our old situations and old memories will haunt us. All of them drag us back instead of moving forward. That is why we remain in the illusion of being the same and not the other. The same effect rubs off on our children. If we always tell our children about our difficulties and try hard, they will not be able to work hard with the same difficulty in mind. They don't even want to think about why it's so difficult. It is better to see what they want now. It is better to leave the old situations and think about what to do now. It would be good if we leave the fact that we have gone through many hardships and think of it as a different experience. Everything is important in life, everything possible should be experienced.

17

Life

To know about life, even if you wait for total life, you will not know anything. And some miracles do not happen. Life is what you see. We are our responsibilities, it is better to think how they are. Having high expectations leads to disillusionment. As long as one is in disillusionment, certain realities cannot be recognized.

Topic-2: No one knows where life is, why life is, why life dissolves. Those elusive thoughts are always haunting. We must always answer them with something or else we feel something is in danger. All of them are unspeakable and meaningless. If we ask anyone else.. their situation is the same as ours. Still no one has any clarity. But for them, they are making something. On the outside, they look like they mean something normal. Some people seem to know everything. But for everyone, from time to time empires built on some unbearable reality crumble and start anew. But they are all thoughts. Life is not an idea, nor is it something that can be discovered from yet formed ideas. Life is beyond thought, not controlled by thought, unrelated to thought. We are thinking because we have the power of thinking. Things don't stop but facts don't change.

Topic-3: Life is like a great stream, but we make and live like a small channel.

Topic-4: The people we admire the most, and our enemies all together, are no more than ten. But our whole life our thoughts revolve around them. How are all our thoughts? We feel that we need to be approved by someone, and we are doing all our work for them, and we are living for them. They are the reason why most of our work is done. And they are also the reason why our work is stopped. We spend our whole life thinking about small reasons. If you think about all this life will be so short?. Or are we making ourselves too small? It seems We sometimes unknowingly set some boundaries and think that life is too small. But life is many times greater than what we think, and beyond all this. If it makes sense then it will be known. Then it will be different.

Topic-5: Only those who are ahead in a task and those who have achieved something do not have a good understanding of life. They may have talent for that job but life is the same for everyone. Awareness of life is very important for everyone regardless of what they have achieved or not. Finally, if you think that something is missed, then there is nothing.

Topic-6: It is good if the purpose of motivation is to create awareness about life. Otherwise it is of no use to tell all the information we know that we cannot follow regardless of the situation. It will be of no use if the listeners expect something too much and collect information without understanding it. When the real danger comes, the information we have put together will not work. Then there is no time to remember and follow.. What we understand is inbuilt in our mind. That's why it's important to understand everything and then do the same.

18

Love

Loving someone or some is not love, if your heart is filled with love, it affects everyone... family members, everything, everything we do. Or if you want to lock it in a box and leave it on someone, or on some, or on some... it is not possible because it does not exist in such a place. Even truth cannot be locked up and used, otherwise it would not be there.

Topic-2: We think about some of them and name them as love and some of them as success. But that is not the property to achieve success. You can make any effort about love, write any poetry about love, sing any number of songs, but that is not love. And it is not something that we can imagine in our favor, or something that grows gradually. Mother's love for children is not achieved or gradually increased and became successful. It will be. That's it. Thinking as needed, being as needed is not love. How long is our quarrel but where is the love in it?. No matter how hard you try, it will not come. Because there is a motive behind those efforts, it is not all love. That's why if you stop trying and understand what is not, it will be there and come.

The same works on everyone, works on everything, works on doing. Or if you want to lock it in a box and leave it on someone or some people, it is not possible. Because in such a place, it does not exist.

Topic-3: Being too fond, to like more, is only related to ourselves, a characteristic that exists within us. But it may or may not be because of the greatness of the people or things we love. Love is a feeling that develops in our mind. It still likes to be liked in a negative way but still likes not to be liked. Anything grows but external people or things may or may not change accordingly and that's why the things we love change. Then senseless restlessness and suffering are inevitable. Also, anger, jealousy, hatred, desire for revenge, pain, sympathy, and what we think is love are some of the qualities that we have in ourselves. These can also be used outside, but the outside conditions may not be suitable for them. Some expectations keep rising but the external situation does not change according to them. Sometimes, even if other people do not have the great qualities that we like, there is a quality that we feel great about and it works on them. Most of what we create is something that other people have nothing to do with. We create some problems as well. Fans are better than those who are admired, there are no characters that influence us, it is all our creation, if they grow equal to it, it will remain the same, or else other people will come in that place. Movies are also made according to our feelings so we like them very much. The hero is also different from the reality that is not a fan. We have a problem-creating quality that creates problems but originally it is not that much of a problem.

Topic-4: Respecting you is not because you are great.. it is my nature. We don't know why, we have crazy affection, it confuses others, and some of us don't make sense. Our affection has nothing to do with them until we realize.

19

Stories

Example stories just for understanding the mind tricks

Story-1: Wanting is different, being is different: One wants to be an I.A.S officer. But he does not start any work except eating and sleeping every day... and after a few days, the same situation. He does not start any work but keeps thinking that he wants to be an I.A.S officer. Actually being an I.A.S officer is completely different. A lot of planning has to be done for it and a lot of hard work has to be done. After that, a few days pass and how to become an I.A.S officer. He knows that he needs to do a lot of preparation and a lot of hard work. Then he will feel how difficult it is to be. All those things he learned will eventually become very heavy. And then it all becomes too difficult to even think about. Then one day it seems that "wanting rather than being" is much easier. And after that he keeps adjusting with dreams. For a few days those dreams become very important and starting work does not seem so important. He agrees with them that dreams are much easier than being difficult. And many years pass. Yet life comes to an end. Did he do anything at the end of life? Then he realizes. But then there was no time for whatever he wanted to do. Wanting is different, being is different.

Story-2: Honest: A thief is asked who are you? he will answer honestly that I am a thief who commits thefts. A thief tell the truth that I am a thief! Everyone will be surprised! One day, knowing that there are diamonds in a neighboring kingdom, he reaches that kingdom to steal them. There he is perched on the top of a tree and staring at the fort. Just then, the king of that kingdom saw the thief wandering around in disguise to find out about the welfare of the people and asked, "Who are you?" He asks, the thief says that I am a thief, knowing that there are diamonds in this fort, I have come to steal them. Then the king in disguise will be very surprised!. A thief does not mean that he tells the truth that I am a thief. Then the thief tells the king that you stay here and see, I will give you half of those diamonds. Still thinking about it! The existing king agrees to a deal of half a diamond, for a while. Later the thief enters the fort. He approaches the diamonds and notices that there are seven diamonds there. Seven diamonds cannot be divided into half, so he brings only six diamonds and tells the king about it, gives three diamonds and leaves. Then the king sends word to the minister to inspect the diamonds. The minister pockets the single diamond and tells the king that all the diamonds are stolen. The king is suspicious of the minister about that one diamond, and he checks the minister, and that one diamond comes out in the minister's pocket. The king punishes the minister severely, then brings the thief and makes him the minister of his kingdom. Then the king will be very happy. Because nothing happens without his knowledge, because he knows what is still there. Also, if we are honest about our mind, we will know exactly where we are and there will be development.

Story-3: Tough Situations: Sometimes we have to struggle in different ways. It feels very tough and critical to us, and we don't like it at all, but because of such situations, we learn a lot without knowing it. Example Story: - There is one person. He is crazy about martial arts. He searches the whole world for a great teacher to learn martial arts and finally joins a teacher. When will the teacher start the class! He looks forward to it very excitedly. But that teacher is that type. Without starting the class, he always tells various things and puts conditions to do those things according to the method he said. He does not want to put wall paint. If he is applying wall paint, he keeps saying that it is not in clockwise direction.. or in anti clockwise direction.. and it is annoying. Then many days pass, and the teacher says that he does different things every day, but does not start the class. He gets very angry. Day by day it becomes difficult. He doesn't want to go home because there is no profit, but he likes martial arts so he stays hoping to wait a few more days. A few days will pass. Still the same situation is not class start. He will not be disappointed again, this time he will take the decision to go strong and prepare everything. But that day the teacher called him and gave him black belt and black belt certificate. Then he doesn't understand!, Why don't I start the class with the teacher yet? He asks, to which the teacher tells him that you have already learned everything my boy. He was surprised! When asked how the teacher, then the teacher explained all the martial art syllabus in the works he has done. The way he applied wall paint in clockwise direction is called upper block, it is used to block when someone hits him on the head, and the way he applied wall paint in anti-clockwise direction is called lower block, it is used to block when someone hits him in the stomach, and also in all the works he did. Explains total martial arts syllabus. Then he gets total realization and falls at the Guru's feet. After few days he becomes a great fighter. He is very happy.

Printed in Great Britain
by Amazon